UNBREAKABLE SPORTS RECORDS?

SWIMMING RECORDS
THAT WILL BE TOUGH TO BEAT

Carla Mooney

Mitchell Lane
PUBLISHERS

Mitchell Lane
PUBLISHERS

mitchelllanepub.com

2001 SW 31st Avenue
Hallandale, FL 33009

First Edition, 2026.
Author: Carla Mooney
Designer: Ed Morgan
Editor: Tammy Gagne

Series: Unbreakable Sports Records?
Title: Swimming Records That Will Be Tough to Beat

Library bound ISBN: 979-8-89260-727-8
eBook ISBN: 979-8-89260-728-5

Photo credits: cover, p. 13, 15, 17, 19, 27, 31, 33, 35, 45, 49 wikimedia; p. 7, 9, 23, 25 Alamy; p. 37, 41, 43, 51, 53, 55, 56 Shutterstock

CONTENTS

INTRODUCTION

An OLYMPIC RECORD

On July 31, 2021, American swimmer Caeleb Dressel arrived at the Aquatics Centre in Tokyo, Japan. It was the final day of the swimming competition at the 2020 Summer Olympics. The international event had been postponed because of the COVID-19 **pandemic**. Now, a year later, the Tokyo Games were finally being held.

Dressel was ready to swim in the men's 50-meter freestyle final. This race was one length of the Olympic pool. Swimmers dove into the pool from one end and raced to the other. The first swimmer to touch the other side would be the winner.

Dressel was full of nervous energy. He paced back and forth while he waited to go onto the pool deck. Dressel was one of the swimming stars for Team USA. He felt a lot of pressure to swim well.

In Tokyo, Dressel first swam in the men's 4x100-meter freestyle relay. He helped the team win gold in that event. Next, Dressel raced in the men's 100-meter freestyle. He won another gold medal. In the 100-meter butterfly, Dressel won his third gold. He also set a new world record in the race at 49.45 seconds. He and his teammates came in fifth for the 4x100 meter mixed medley final.

American swimmer Caeleb Dressel celebrates after winning a gold medal at the 2020 Summer Olympics in Tokyo, Japan.

Now it was time for the 50-meter final. Dressel stepped onto the starting block. He was in lane four. He leaned over and grabbed the front of the starting block. The buzzer sounded. Dressel exploded into the water. He took the lead immediately. With powerful strokes and kicks, Dressel sprinted across the pool. He touched the wall first in 21.07 seconds. Dressel was 0.48 seconds ahead of the second-place finisher. He won his fourth gold medal at the Tokyo Olympics.

Dressel also set a record. His time was 0.23 seconds faster than the old Olympic record. It was a great race in Olympic swimming. But Dressel was still short of breaking the world record. The world record for the men's 50-meter freestyle remained unbroken.

American swimmer Caeleb Dressel dives with intense focus off the starting block into the pool.

CHAPTER ONE

Most Gold Medals in a Single Olympics—FEMALE SWIMMER

Winning an Olympic medal is the dream of many athletes. Winning a gold medal is even sweeter. Winning six gold medals in a single Olympics was a record-breaking accomplishment for one female swimmer, Germany's Kristin Otto.

Born in 1966, Otto grew up in East Germany. As a child, she showed obvious talent in the pool. At age eleven, a national scouting program selected her to attend a special sports school. There, she trained to become a world-class swimmer.

Otto quickly became a swimming star. The sixteen-year-old swimmer won three gold medals at the 1982 World Championships, including an individual gold in the 100-meter backstroke. At the 1983 European Championships, Otto won three more medals. She was expected to win a medal at the 1984 Olympics in Los Angeles. However, Otto's Olympic dreams were dashed when East Germany **boycotted** the 1984 Games.

Otto faced another hurdle when she cracked a **vertebra** later that year. She had to wear a neck brace for nine months while her body healed. Doctors advised Otto to give up competitive swimming. But Otto refused. She returned to competition at the 1986 World Championships. There, Otto won four gold and two silver medals. She also set a world record in the 100-meter freestyle.

Kristin Otto is regarded as one of the greatest swimmers in the history of the sport.

In 1987, Otto remained spectacular in the pool. She won five gold medals at the European Championships. East Germany's head coach, Wolfgang Richter, spoke about Otto's ability to perform under pressure in an article for *Swimming World Magazine*. "She's the best because she works harder than the rest. She's tough (in the mind). She cannot stand to lose," he said.

The 1988 Olympic Games were held in Seoul, South Korea. In her first swimming event, Otto won gold in the 100-meter freestyle. She won two more gold medals, one in the 100-meter backstroke and the other as part of East Germany's 400-meter freestyle relay. Otto added two more individual gold medals in the 100-meter butterfly and the 50-meter freestyle.

The East German coaches now had a decision to make. Otto had won gold in every 100-meter race at the 1988 Olympics. The coaches had to decide what stroke she would swim in the medley relay: backstroke, breaststroke, butterfly, or freestyle. They decided Otto would start the race with the backstroke. Otto and her team won the race. She won her sixth gold medal.

Kornelia Ender

Whose Record Did Otto Beat?

At the 1976 Montreal Olympics, East German swimmer Kornelia Ender won four gold medals. She won the 100-meter freestyle, the 200-meter freestyle, the 100-meter butterfly, and the 4x100-meter medley relay. It was a record-setting performance. Ender was the first female swimmer to win four golds at a single Olympics. Her record lasted more than a decade until fellow East German swimmer Kristin Otto broke it in 1988.

CHAPTER ONE

Kristin Otto was the first female athlete to win six gold medals at a single Summer Olympic Games. Otto later said in a *New York Times* article that she had not entered the Games thinking about gold medals. "I never give much thought to that because it would be so much of a burden if I expected gold in every race," she said. Otto's record of six gold medals in a single Olympics remains unbroken.

Some people believe that the East German athletes of Otto's era benefited from performance-enhancing drugs. Otto never tested positive for any banned substance. She has consistently denied ever knowingly taking one. However, team officials confessed years later to a **doping** program. The officials claimed they gave performance-enhancing drugs to Otto. As she never tested positive for banned drugs, Otto has kept her Olympic medals and record.

East German Kristen Otto looks up and smiles after finishing one of her many races in the pool.

Torri Huske

Chasing Otto's Record

American swimmer Torri Huske is a two-time Olympian. Her first Olympic appearance was at the 2020 Tokyo Games. Huske swam in several races and won a silver medal in the 4x100-meter medley relay. At the 2024 Paris Olympics, Huske competed in five events and medaled in each. She won three golds and two silvers in the pool. Huske is looking forward to the 2028 Olympics in Los Angeles, California. If she adds one more event to her swimming line-up, Huske could be on track to match Otto's gold medal record.

CHAPTER TWO

Fastest 50-METER FREESTYLE

The 50-meter freestyle race is a furious dash across the pool. The long course version of this race is one length across an Olympic-sized pool. The athlete who touches the wall first is known as the fastest swimmer in the world. César Cielo has held the record for this event for more than a decade.

CHAPTER TWO

Cielo was born in Brazil in 1987. His mother was a physical education teacher who also taught swimming at a local club. Cielo quickly took to the water. In 2004, he was the fastest Brazilian swimmer in the fifteen to sixteen age group.

At eighteen, Cielo moved to the United States to join the Auburn University swim team. He quickly advanced to become one of the world's fastest freestyle sprint swimmers. At the 2008 Beijing Olympics, twenty-one-year-old Cielo won a bronze medal in the 100-meter freestyle.

Next up was the 50-meter freestyle. Cielo raced well in the **preliminary** and semifinal rounds. Now, he stepped onto the starting block for the final. As the starting gun sounded, Cielo dove into the pool. He sprinted to the other side in a winning time of 21.30 seconds. After the race, Cielo was emotional as he described his feelings. "I did it. It was my best race ever. Today was my lucky day. The sun shone on me. I'm so overwhelmed with emotion. I gave up a lot for this medal. I never saw my family," he said.

César Cielo celebrates after winning the men's 50-meter freestyle at the 2008 Beijing Olympics.

The following year, Cielo swam an even better race. In December 2009, he broke the world record in the 50-meter freestyle. He swam the race in 20.91 seconds at a meet in Sao Paulo, Brazil. Cielo also set the world record in the 100-meter freestyle at 46.91 seconds in July 2009. "This year has been a year to remember for me. I'm going to save it as a **template** for the rest of my career," Cielo said in an ESPN interview.

Frédérick Bousquet

Whose Record Did Cielo Beat?

Before 2009, no swimmer had finished the 50-meter freestyle in less than 21 seconds. Then, in April 2009, French swimmer Frédérick Bousquet broke the 21-second barrier. His time of 20.94 became a new world record. However, Bousquet could only enjoy his time as a world record holder for a few months. By December 2009, Cielo broke the record by three-hundredths of a second.

Cielo wore a high-tech swimsuit for both his world-record swims. The suits were developed before the 2008 Beijing Games. They were made of non-textile materials such as **polyurethane** and designed to reduce drag in the water. With less resistance, swimmers could move faster. However, many people believed the high-tech suits gave an unfair advantage to larger swimmers. World Aquatics banned the use of these high-tech suits beginning in 2010.

Since 2009, Cielo's world record in the 100-meter freestyle has been broken. However, no one has matched his performance in the 50-meter freestyle. He remains the world's fastest swimmer.

Cameron McEvoy

Chasing Cielo's Record

Australian swimmer Cameron McEvoy earned the title of fastest swimmer in the world at the 2024 Paris Summer Olympics. McEvoy won the gold medal in the 50-meter freestyle race with a time of 21.25. The win was McEvoy's first Olympic gold medal. His best in the 50-meter freestyle is 21.06, which he swam in the 2023 World Championship finals.

CHAPTER THREE

Most OLYMPIC GOLD MEDALS

For Michael Phelps, winning medals comes naturally. The American swimming legend has twenty-eight Olympic medals, twenty-three of them gold. Phelps has more than twice as many gold medals as any other Olympian. He is considered one of the greatest Olympians in history.

CHAPTER THREE

Phelps grew up in Baltimore, Maryland. At age seven, he joined the North Baltimore Aquatic Club. By age fifteen, Phelps was swimming at the 2000 Sydney Games, his first Olympics. He was the youngest male swimmer on the team in nearly seventy years. Although Phelps won no medals in Sydney, the teenager gained valuable experience.

Phelps won six gold medals at the 2004 Athens Olympics. He also won two bronze medals. Phelps' six gold medals was one short of the record for a single Olympic Games.

Four years later, Phelps broke that record. At the 2008 Beijing Games, Phelps won a record eight gold medals. He took gold in every race he entered and set seven world records. Phelps spoke about his Beijing experience in an article for *The New York Times*. "This is all a dream come true. Doing all best times. Winning every race. Everything was accomplished that I wanted to do. It's been one fun week, that's for sure," he said.

MOST OLYMPIC GOLD MEDALS

Michael Phelps's twenty-three gold medals may be the toughest record for another athlete—in any sport—to beat.

CHAPTER THREE

Phelps's dominance in the pool continued at the 2012 London Olympics. There, he won four more gold medals and two silver medals. At the end of the London Games, Phelps considered retiring. However, he decided to return one more time for the 2016 Rio de Janeiro Olympics.

In Rio, Phelps was golden in the pool again. He added five more gold medals and one more silver to his collection. His final Olympic race was the 4x100 medley relay. Phelps swam butterfly for the third leg. He entered the water in second place. By the time he finished his 100 meters, Team USA was in first place. The final U.S. swimmer, Nathan Adrian, held the lead to win the gold for the United States. It was Phelps's twenty-third Olympic gold medal and twenty-eighth medal overall.

Mark Spitz

Whose Record Did Phelps Beat?

Before Michael Phelps, Mark Spitz was known as the greatest Olympic swimmer. At the 1968 Mexico City Olympic Games, Spitz won two gold medals in relay races. However, he was disappointed not to win any of his individual races. At the 1972 Munich Olympics, Spitz found redemption. He raced in seven events and won gold in each. He also set a world record in all seven races. Spitz held the record for the most gold medals won at a single Olympics, with seven. He also set a record for the most gold medals of any Olympic athlete, with nine. His records lasted for nearly four decades until Phelps broke both.

CHAPTER THREE

John Lohn is a **correspondent** for *Swimming World Magazine*. He has followed Phelps' career since the Olympian was fifteen years old. Lohn described Phelps's competitive drive in an interview with CNN. "It doesn't matter if he's got one, nineteen, or twenty-three gold medals, he doesn't think like that. He thinks like he's trying to win his first medal. He has a competitive switch you only see in very few people. Michael Jordan had it . . . that killer instinct," said Lohn.

Michael Phelps is widely considered the greatest swimmer and one of the greatest athletes ever. Phelps dominated swimming for nearly twenty years. He singlehandedly brought global interest to the sport of swimming. Phelps is the most decorated Olympian of all time. His gold medal record stands unbroken.

Michael Phelps extends his arms and takes a breath as he makes swimming the butterfly stroke look easy.

CHAPTER THREE

Chasing Phelps's Record

Léon Marchand is a rising star in the swimming world. He trains with Michael Phelps's former coach. The twenty-two-year-old French swimmer competed in his first Olympics in Paris in 2024. He won four gold medals and one bronze. In his races, Marchand set several Olympic records. In the 400-meter individual medley, Marchand set a new world record. He broke Michael Phelps's world record by more than one second. At the Paris medal ceremony, Phelps awarded Marchand with his gold medal for his record-breaking win.

Léon Marchand

CHAPTER FOUR

Most WORLD Championships INDIVIDUAL TITLES

The world's top swimmers compete for more than Olympic gold medals. They also swim in the World Aquatic Championships. The World Championships were first held in 1973. At first, the meet was held every four years. In 1988, the event began taking place every two years.

No swimmer has stood at the top of the podium at the World Championships more than American Katie Ledecky. She has sixteen world individual championship titles. She also has five relay gold medals and five silver medals.

Ledecky began swimming around age six. She looked up to her mother, who swam in college. Ledecky quickly became a standout in the pool. In high school, she broke several U.S. records. She also earned a swimming scholarship to Stanford University.

When she was fifteen, Ledecky swam in her first Olympics, the 2012 London Games. She won her first gold medal in the 800-meter freestyle. After London, Ledecky swam in three more Olympic Games, including the 2024 Paris Games. She has won a total of fourteen Olympic medals. Nine of them are gold.

MOST WORLD CHAMPIONSHIP INDIVIDUAL TITLES

At fifteen years of age, Katie Ledecky was the youngest athlete on the 2012 U.S. Olympic swimming team.

CHAPTER FOUR

When not winning Olympic medals, Ledecky was dominating the World Championships. At the 2023 World Aquatic Championships in Japan, Ledecky won her 16th individual world title in the 800-meter freestyle, her signature race. With sixteen individual world titles, Ledecky broke the record held by Michael Phelps.

Ledecky's win in the 800-meter freestyle was her sixth **consecutive** win in that event. She set another record as the first swimmer to win six consecutive titles in the same event. In more than a decade, Ledecky has not lost the 800-meter freestyle. Ledecky shared in a CBS News article that the 800-meter freestyle is her favorite race. "It's just the one that I hold closest to me, given that the 1500 was only added to the Olympics in 2021. I think it's the one I've focused on the most," she said.

Michael Phelps

Whose Record Did Ledecky Beat?

Michael Phelps is viewed by many as the greatest swimmer of all time. Phelps is the most decorated Olympian, with twenty-three gold medals. He also has twenty-six world championship gold medals. Fifteen of Phelps's world championship titles are in individual events. He won his fifteenth individual event in 2011. He held the record for the most individual world championship titles for over a decade until Katie Ledecky broke it in 2023.

At the 2023 World Championships, Ledecky also won gold in the 1500-meter freestyle. It was her fifth consecutive title in that event. Ledecky spoke about her world championship records in a CBS News article. She explained how her fellow swimmers have pushed her to give her best in the pool. "I've never even dreamt of even coming to meets like this, so to be here and to have been to a bunch of world championships is amazing. It is always a battle, it is always a great race. So I know I have to bring my best every single time," she said.

Ledecky has earned her place as one of the world's greatest swimmers. As of 2024, she holds the world record in the 800-meter and 1500-meter freestyle. She is also the most decorated female swimmer of all time, with thirty-three golds, twelve silvers, and one bronze in Olympic and international swimming competitions.

Sarah Sjöström

Chasing Ledecky's Record

Sarah Sjöström became the first Swedish female swimmer to win Olympic gold. She won the 100-meter butterfly at the 2016 Rio Games. In 2024, she added two more golds in the 50-meter freestyle and the 100-meter freestyle in Paris. As of 2024, Sjöström has won fourteen individual gold medals at the World Aquatic Championships. She has also won six world titles in the same event, the 50-meter butterfly.

CHAPTER FIVE

Fastest 1500-Meter FREESTYLE

The 1500-meter freestyle is the longest swimming event in the pool. Swimmers complete thirty laps in an Olympic-sized pool. The race is a grueling test of a swimmer's endurance and **stamina**. U.S. swimmer Bobby Finke holds the record for the fastest time in this event.

Bobby Finke was born in 1999 into a family of swimmers. His mother swam in college, and his father is a respected swim coach at St. Petersburg Aquatics in Florida. His two older sisters also swam in college and competed nationally.

CHAPTER FIVE

Finke followed his family into the pool. He quickly established himself as a talented swimmer who **specialized** in long-distance races. Finke broke the state championship age group records for the 800-meter and 1500-meter freestyle at fourteen years old. He earned a scholarship to swim at the University of Florida. Finke won the 2021 national championship for the 400-meter individual medley and 1650-meter freestyle in college. He repeated as the 1,650-meter national champion in 2022.

Finke's first Olympic appearance was at the 2020 Tokyo Games. He did not expect a medal. In his first final, the 800-meter freestyle, Finke swam in fifth place for most of the race. Then, in the final 50 meters, Finke blasted through the water. He touched the wall first and won his first Olympic gold medal. A few days later, Finke won again in the 1500-meter freestyle. Once again, he turned up his speed in the final 50 meters to finish first. It was the first gold medal for the USA men in the 1500 race since 1984.

FASTEST 1500-METER FREESTYLE

Bobby Finke's first Olympic appearance was at the 2020 Tokyo Games. They were held in 2021 due to the COVID-19 pandemic.

After his races, Finke admitted he was surprised by the results in an article for the Associated Press News. "Honestly, it doesn't seem too real. I came in not expecting to medal and just do my best to make the finals. To come out with two golds, it means the world to me and my family and my teammates," he said.

After the 2020 Tokyo Games, Finke's rivals were ready for fast finishes. But at the 2023 World Championships, Finke was out-touched for the gold medal in the 1500-meter freestyle. At the 2024 Paris Olympics, Ireland's Daniel Wiffen was able to hold off Finke in the 800-meter freestyle. Finke captured the silver medal.

FASTEST 1500-METER FREESTYLE

Sun Yang

Whose Record Did Finke Beat?

In 2012, Sun Yang won China's first Olympic gold medal in men's swimming. At the London Games, he won gold in the 400-meter and 1500-meter freestyle races. He set a world record in the 1500-meter race. Four years later, Yang won Olympic gold again in the 200-meter freestyle at the 2016 Rio Games. However, Yang's career has been clouded with **controversy**. He was banned for four years from international swimming after refusing to cooperate with a drug test. Because Yang never tested positive for a banned substance, he was allowed to keep his medals.

CHAPTER FIVE

Finke still had the 1500-meter freestyle final on the last day of the Olympic swimming competition. He hoped the longer distance would work to his advantage. After the first 50 meters, Finke was in first place. He kept his lead for the rest of the race. "That really was not my strategy to go into the race. I didn't know how the race was going to play out, so I kind of saw I had a pretty decent lead at the 300, and I knew I kind of just had to keep going and hopefully try and make the guys hurt a little bit trying to catch up to me," Finke said in a *Swimming World Magazine* article.

Bobby Finke swims the men's 1,500-meter freestyle at the 2024 Paris Summer Olympics.

For much of the race, Finke was also swimming faster than the world record pace. China's Sun Yang had set the 1500-meter world record in 2012 at 14:31.02. Finke kept pushing in the final lengths of the race. He finished in first place with a time of 14:30:67. It was a new world record.

Some swimming records stand for just weeks or months. A new record may be just hundredths of a second faster than the previous one, but this tiny fraction is enough to place a new swimmer in the record books. Other records have cemented athletes in the history books for years or even decades, unlikely to be replaced anytime soon.

Bobby Finke shows off his gold and silver medals from the 2024 Paris Olympic Games.

Daniel Wiffen

Chasing Finke's Record

Daniel Wiffen is a champion Irish swimmer. At the 2024 Paris Games, Wiffen beat Bobby Finke in the 800-meter freestyle to win the gold. He set an Olympic record in the race. In the 1500-meter freestyle, Wiffen won the bronze medal. His time of 14:39.63 was just nine seconds behind Bobby Finke's world record.

Think FAST!

Test your new knowledge of swimming by answering the following questions.

1. How often are the Olympic Games held?
2. What are the four swimming strokes in the Olympics?
3. What is a medley relay in swimming?
4. What title does the winner of the 50-meter freestyle earn?
5. How many gold medals does Michael Phelps have?
6. How many Olympic Games did Michael Phelps swim in?
7. What race is Katie Ledecky's favorite?
8. How many times has Katie Ledecky won the 800-meter freestyle at the World Championships?
9. During which Olympics did Bobby Finke win his first gold medal?
10. Who held the 1500-meter freestyle world record before Bobby Finke?

Answer Key 1. Every four years 2. Freestyle, backstroke, butterfly, and breaststroke 3. A race in which four swimmers take turns swimming different strokes 4. The fastest swimmer in the world 5. 23 6. Five: 2000 Sydney, 2004 Athens, 2008 Beijing, 2012 London, 2026 Rio 7. 800-meter freestyle 8. Six 9. The 2020 Tokyo Games 10. China's Sun Yang

Glossary

boycotted
Refused to participate as a form of protest

consecutive
Directly following another instance

controversy
A topic known for opposing viewpoints

correspondent
A news reporter for a magazine, television station, or other media outlet

doping
The unlawful use of drugs to improve an athlete's performance

pandemic
A disease outbreak occurring over a wide geographical area

polyurethane
A plastic material that can be used in waterproofing

preliminary
Occurring before another event

specialized
Focused on a particular area of competition

stamina
The ability to endure prolonged mental or physical stress

template
An approach that serves as a guide for future success

vertebra
One of the bones that form the spine

Find Out More

IN PRINT

Hecht, Micah. *Who Is Michael Phelps?* Penguin Workshop, 2024.

McDougall, Chrös. *The Olympics Encyclopedia*. Abdo, 2022.

Mooney, Carla. *Hockey Records That Will Be Tough to Beat*. Mitchell Lane Publishers, 2026.

ON THE INTERNET

***ESPN*, n.d.**
www.espn.com.

***Olympics*, n.d.**
https://olympics.com/en.

***World Aquatics*, n.d.**
www.worldaquatics.com.

Index

About the Author

Carla Mooney is the author of many books for young adults and children. She lives in Pittsburgh, Pennsylvania, with her husband and three children. She enjoys watching the Summer Olympics every four years.